Willi Darr

Conception for Procurement Excellence

The performance profile and degree of digitalization of procurement

Willi Darr

Conception for Procurement Excellence

The performance profile and degree of
digitalization of procurement

tredition Verlag
Hamburg

Prof. Dr. Willi Darr

University of Applied Sciences Hof

Procurement and Logistics Management

Alfons-Goppel-Platz1 ı D-95028 Hof/ Saale

Hardcover   ISBN 978-3-7482-6475-0
Paperback   ISBN 978-3-7482-6474-3
E-Book   ISBN 978-3-7482-6476-7

Bibliografische Information der Deutschen Nationalbibliothek

Die Deutsche Nationalbibliothek verzeichnet diese Publikation in der Deutschen Nationalbibliografie; detaillierte biblio-grafische Daten sind im Internet über http://dnb.dnb.de abrufbar.

Cover and design by tredition & Willi Darr

Herstellung und Verlag ı Printed and published by

tredition GmbH, Halenreie 40-44, D-22359 Hamburg, Germany

Preface

The subject of this book is Procurement Excellence (the excellence of purchasing management) of procuring companies which is deemed a highly relevant topic out of two reasons.

Firstly, corporate procurement, respectively purchasing management has witnessed a significant boost of importance over the last years. Increased outsourcing of services to suppliers and, simultaneously, commissioning of international subcontractors, have heavily altered the responsibilities and job description of purchasers with regards to their contribution to the company's added value. Additionally, product developments along (global) supply chains are growing steadily. Meaning that without excellent supply chain management by the company's purchasing departments, corporate strategies can no longer be executed, or competitive advantages sustainably realized.

On the other hand, digitalization displays future-oriented alternatives for corporate added value and hence provides fundamental opportunities and necessities to reach and sustain (global) competitiveness. Logically, these developments shape the quality of procurement and its processes to suppliers. This means in turn that without excellence of management quality, corporate strategies cannot be implemented, nor competitive advantages sustainably obtained.

Only an excellent purchasing department can be an authentic success indicator within a company. This book focuses on the two pillars of Procurement Excellence. To do so, a conception for categorizing and controlling purchasing performances, and a conception for categorizing digitalization will be illustrated in order to make differentiated statements regarding Procurement Excellence. Its two related dimensions will be merged within a final overall statement regarding Procurement Excellence.

These insights have great advantages for all interested parties: (i) Each particular profile and detailed knowledge of the degree of digitalization allow for the *responsible parties of the purchasing department* to directly decide over an examination and extension of services, respectively the digitalization. Understanding their own Procurement Excellence is the foundation of the next purchasing strategy. (ii) *Research and teaching* will benefit from adopting authentically practicable concepts as basics for education and training. (iii) *Students* of the subjects Purchase, Supply Chain or Logistics benefit from obtaining practicable tools for their own purposes in later life.

In order to preserve legibility, the publication does not include references to male or female individuals.

Special thanks to Mrs. Mai Beck who has translated my German book into the English language.

To all interested readers I wish lots of helpful ideas and insights.

Prof. Dr. Willi Darr

Table of Contents

List of Figures

List of Tables

1. Introductory Thoughts

Procurement and its services are (broadly) acknowledged as equal part of a company's added value by process reliability, earnings and risk management and profiling in the sales market. However, the level of realization of this equality within companies has not yet been consistently implemented. These development processes are currently taking place. They can and will be initiated, facilitated and expedited by a convincing performance, respectively excellence of procurement.

Today, purchasing management is operating within an unstable and complex environment: Political, ecological, social and technological conditions build a challenging framework for responsible parties of the purchasing department in companies. The mostly global playing field boasts fast and innovative competitors. Hence, responsible parties of the purchasing department are dealing with an entire bundle of simultaneous developments on their agenda. It is even more important that each responsible of the purchasing department is able to assess the range of services of „his" purchasing department in detail in order to design a success formula (meaning strategies and measures) that is compliant with the target of the corporate strategy. The focus of this Procurement Excellence book is the transparent current range of services and design of the future-viability of the purchasing management. It should clarify and help find rough approaches of further development (strategy).

For this purpose, two foundations will be outlined in the beginning: on the one hand, section 2 will explain different ranges of services in purchasing by the dimensions of Utility (N) and User (R), in order to categorize the services of purchasing clearly and unambiguously. This possibly includes designing key performance indicators (KPIs) to illustrate and measure these services. On the other hand, section 3 will outline different forms of digitalization of activities in purchasing because they represent the support of its management quality to a high degree. They will be explained and categorized by different information products/states of digitalization. Finally, the book will conclude by integrating the two dimensions of Procurement Excellence and by displaying development trajectories, respectively strategies.

2. Groundwork 1: User and Utility of Purchasing Services

a. Basic Idea

The basic idea of analyzing purchasing services assumes that they are describable in a one-to-one manner and delimitable from each other. Individual and conceptually incoherent statements in terms of a „long list" are of no help in this matter. And a very reduced argument stating that purchasing must essentially decrease material and procurement costs will no longer do the purchasing department as a value adding area of the company justice. Bearing in mind the from all sides emphasized growing, respectively strategic importance of the purchasing department, or rather purchasing services, it is to note critically that central text books lack or merely outline conceptions as such to some extent. The works of Heß (2010), Lysons/Farrington (2012), Krampf (2014), Large (2014), Bailey et al. (2015) and van Weele/Eßig (2017) are named as examples. Hence, this work will briefly explain Users and Utility of purchasing services first.

b. Forms of Utility and Users of Purchasing Services

The conception of measuring purchasing services is based on the differentiation of Users (R) and Utility (N), (see Darr, 2017b and 2019).

(1) To begin with, **Users** (R) are addressed. From the vantage point of view of a purchasing company, three main Users (Recipients) of the purchasing service are differentiated: purchasing, production and sales. **Production,** as a classic User of procurement of purchasing goods, is the focus. The differentiating explanation of purchasing non-production materials or investment

goods is deliberately abandoned at this point. Production is provided preliminary products in an organized fashion by suppliers and purchasing, so that the use of external procurement always (ought to) exceeds the use of in-house produce. In a classic manner, production is the Key User of purchasing services because here the offered product is manufactured specifically. **Purchasing** being the second User, the phase prior to production is referred to without having direct services performed for production. This preliminary phase contains benefit components that are created for the company; however, they do not impact production. Here, facilitations in the goods receipt **(WE)** or an optimized capital commitment through lower purchase prices are a few to mention. **Sales** as third User assesses those purchasing services which are created after completion of production, and which particularly influence the sales process and therefore the customers of the purchasing company immediately. This way for instance, end customer assessments can be directly shaped by recognizable preliminary products of suppliers (i.e., Ingredient Brands, such as Intel Inside or Goretex).

The recipient of purchasing services defines the **profundity of effects** of purchasing services for external services. With its services, purchasing can exert influence not only upon sections within production, but also upon sections prior to and post production. Table 2.1 illustrates this with individual examples.

This division into three Users is now further refined. Within each profundity, three aspects are differentiated by which the Benefit of purchasing service can unfold: services through a better **provision** by the upstream step; services through facilitations in the **processing** of each section of the supply chain; through a facilitated **transfer** to the next step of the supply chain.

Profundity of effects ,until purchasing'	Profundity of effects ,until production'	Profundity of effects ,until sales'
Examples	Examples	Examples
• Low purchasing prices • Easy to open goods-receipt-packaging • Coordinated delivery in the goods receipt without congestions • Online transmission of master data of purchasing goods	• Supply of required parts • Production-synchronized supply of goods and prevention of intermediate storages • Assurance of confirmed quality of procured goods	• Offering end customer-relevant components of suppliers • Rapidness of spare parts supply • No scandals, through complete transparency and compliance in the supply chain

Table 2.1: Profundity of effects of purchasing services

With that, purchasing services can impact three aspects of each supply chain step: input, process/throughout or output. The dimensions by which the service will be measured will be briefly discussed in the following. When applied to the three Users of purchasing services, these three fundamental forms of unfolding benefit will result in a final categorizing overview of Users of purchasing services (see table 2.2).

Users **prior** to production (in purchasing)	Users **within** production (in manufacturing)	Users **after** production (in sales)
• Facilitated input through the suppliers, and for purchasing • Facilitated processing in purchasing and in the goods receipt • Facilitated output of purchasing for production	• Facilitated output of purchasing for production • Facilitated processing in production • Facilitated output of production for sales	• Facilitated input for sales • Facilitated processing of sales • Facilitated output of sales for customers

Table 2.2: Categories of Users of purchasing services

Thereby, output of purchasing and input of production are equated. This is also true for output of production and input of sales.

(2) Now, the dimensions of **Benefit** (N) are made subject, and therefore the importance of purchasing services. The background is built by the foundation of Benefit as business administrative dimension.

A company's *added value* is based fundamentally on its buyers', respectively customers', *appreciation* of services. This appreciation is expressed in the acceptance of said services compared to competitors' services and is manifested in the exchange relationships of entrepreneurial services (products/ services) and price. Strictly said, a company only occurs costs by combining most different resources to produce unique services. It is not until afterwards, meaning after the appreciation by customers and the exchange of product services and price, that price, preliminary corporate services through suppliers and the company's own manufacturing costs should then result in a positive difference within the framework of internal value adding. With regards to the strategic arrangement of product services, however, the corporate performance profile should be sharply refined, so that the uniqueness of services represents the foundation of a sustained corporate development.

The guideline to this customer- or rather market-oriented corporate leadership, is reflected in *marketing philosophy* and in *marketing management*, respectively. Michael E. *Porter* has formed this aspect through his works on competitive strategy impressively in the 1980s (Porter, 1980). Some time ago, *Kim and Mauborgne* have undertaken further developments with their works to ‚Blue Ocean' by differentiating individual lifecycle phases of the buying and using phase on the one hand, and basic benefit categories on the other hand, in a *Buyer Utility Map* (see Kim/Mauborgne, 2005, p. 109 ff.).

Transferred to purchasing services, three categories of Benefit are distinguished in the following:

- Necessary services with a process benefit
- Important services with an earnings benefit
- Strategic services with a customer benefit

Necessary services set the requirements for the process step in the supply chain. If not self-provided by the organization, these services are to be procured. The supply of goods for the next step is a necessary service. It is to be guaranteed within quality and supply service (i.e., punctuality), in order to prevent interruptions in the value adding process. By doing so, a process benefit is being generated. By doing so, a process benefit is generated.

In the following, **important** services, however, will be defined by their effects on the company's result optimization. Thereby, important services influence the entrepreneurial performance regarding costs, turnover and risks. Furthermore, necessary services can be critical when permanently absent, particularly when mentionable opportunity costs ensue from an interruption.

Strategic services are defined by their influence on the value adding of the belonging company, that means on the value adding of the customers of the belonging company. These so-called strategic purchasing services directly influence the unique selling proposition (USP) towards the customer and the position against the competitors' services. When developed heavily, important services may turn into strategic services - especially, if very positive/negative effects of a purchasing service result in competitively strategic consequences.

Table 2.3 illustrates examples for the three categories of Benefit.

Necessary services	Important services	Strategic services
<ul><li>Safeguarding the purchasing processes</li><li>Safeguarding the required readiness for delivery for production</li><li>Safety within all purchasing and logistics processes</li><li>Safeguarding the delivery of spare parts by suppliers</li><li>Influence on process safety, i.e. under extreme environmental conditions</li></ul>	<ul><li>Influence on the earnings driver, i.e. through excellent quality services</li><li>Influence on the risk driver, i.e. through environmental risks</li><li>Influence on the cost driver, i.e. through procurement prices/exchange rates</li><li>Necessary services that boast a mentionable earnings driver</li></ul>	<ul><li>Influence on the strategic success factors at the customers of the purchasing company (USP)</li><li>Influence on the company's performance on competitors</li><li>Influence on market position, e.g. in the event of limited compliance</li><li>Important services that directly influence the USP</li></ul>

Table 2.3: Examples for the three benefit categories of purchasing services

(3) Now, both dimensions of purchasing services, namely ‚User' and ‚Benefit', are merged. By doing so, a **3x3 matrix** is created and used as a final conceptional frame for the systematization of purchasing services (see table 2.4).

Based on this groundwork, the decision maker can define their as-is profile of the purchasing service for a specific case. In the following, exemplary forms if each particular service is briefly outlined. This way, **traditional** purchasing exclusively performs a necessary service for purchasing and production - without support services for their own production, without cooperation services in the supply chain, without end customer-relevant components and without risk policy. Thereby, a necessary service must be disclosed out of the supply of purchasing goods for production. There are no further existent services in this case.

3x3 matrix		User (R)		
		Purchasing	Production	Sales
Benefit (N)	strategic	Strategic important services for purchasing	Strategic important services for production	Strategic important services for sales
	important	Important services for purchasing	Important services for production	Important services for sales
	necessary	Necessary services for purchasing	Necessary services for production	Necessary services for sales

Table 2.4: Conceptional frame of purchasing services

Set against this, Just-in-time delivery contains an **important** Benefit (earnings benefit) for production, via cost effects within its own production (reduced storage costs, reduced assembly costs) and a seasoned risk management (i.e., in terms of raw material prices).

The third example is represented by the retail purchasers' work on product range. Here, an entirely different profile of purchasing services is displayed since the direct customer and competitive position delivers **strategic** services for the retailer's own sales department, as well. Strategic services maintain in industrial companies if unique product services are performed with/within the supply chain.

The comparison of these three examples is illustrated in figure 2.1. The Benefit profile for the particular Users purchasing (E), production (P) and sales (V) in the Benefit levels strategic (s), important (w) and necessary (n) is expressed by hatched fields.

9

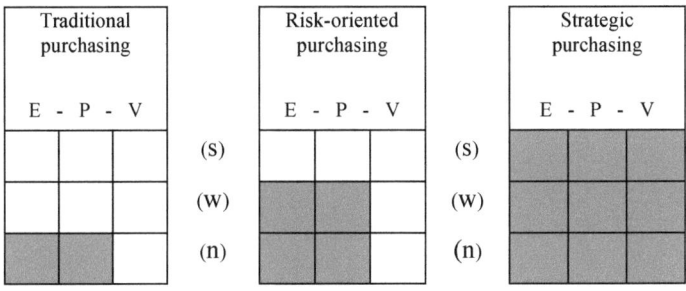

Figure 2.1: Comparison of three profiles for purchasing services

(4) This Benefit profile builds the groundwork for the **key figures'** system of purchasing services. By using these service profiles of Users and Benefit, concrete key figures can be designed to measure the service in the three measure points (input, throughput, output) in the following. These key figures or indicators, respectively, can basically adopt the following **four dimensions**:

- **Volume** key figures (i.e., number of purchasing goods)

- **Time** key figures (i.e., process,/throughput/waiting time)

- **Quality** key figures (i.e., share of error-free processing)

- **Value** key figures (i.e., unit costs or error costs)

This previous system, containing for instance three Users, three starting points per User, three dimensions of Benefit and four dimensions of measuring, mathematically produces a multitude of possible key figures (here: $108 = 3 \times 3 \times 3 \times 4$). This system is helpful by enabling a differentiated categorization of services without overlap and offering a variety of possible types of key figures. The operator can individually elaborate and assess their as-is situation with regards to relevance and completeness. There are therefore sufficient opportunities to examine the interrogations.

c. First interim conclusion

Purchasing services will be based on three Users (R) and three Benefit levels (N) in order to determine the particular corporate situation through interrogations. For each respective profile of purchasing services, the current arrangement of controlling these services is questioned. This again will be determined by the existence and use of key figures (KPIs).

3. Groundwork 2: Scaling of digitalization
a. Digitalization as strategic necessity

The terms „Digitalization" and „4.0" are nowadays self-evident features of all discussions concerning the futures of industry and society. This is content-wise related to the increase in global competitiveness. These terms count as dominant magic formula of the future. Any discussion at congresses, in specialist journals or in public debates about competitiveness that does not include digitalization/4.0, would lose its claim to modernity and future viability.

Viewed from an industrial nation's perspective, it is small wonder that the discussion has been started with the ‚industry 4.0'. However, today, the addition 4.0 is no longer exclusively applied to industrial manufacturing. By now, all areas of life are attributed this modern additional feature. This work examines purchasing or the purchasing management, respectively, in terms of their digital arrangement.

Developing a value chain 4.0 with purchasing 4.0 is in reality not yet a normality. A restrained implementation is still opposing the intense discussion of importance. The lack of practical forming still has future 4.0 arrangements seem risky, so that leaders still lack or haven't yet further developed experience and know how hereto. This tension field between wishing and reality is expressed in all extreme facets (i.e. in Darr, 2017d, S. 3). Indeed, this tension field requires a conceptional discussion to close the gap and to not jeopardize the company's efficiency of the value chain by bottlenecks in the purchasing management.

b. Industry 4.0 as stimulating force

The central features of a new competitive strategy by digitalization have been derived from the developments of Industry 4.0 (the fourth industrial revolution). After the mechanical loom in 1784 (Industry 1.0), after the division of labor in the form of the assembly line (Industry 2.0) and after the development of electronics at the beginning of the 1970s, or the automatization of manufacturing (Industry 3.0), respectively, the next quantum leap of value chain efficiency is attributed to Industry 4.0.

The development towards Industry 4.0 will be expressed hereby by *several technical* features of data collection and processing, with a view to self-controlling the value adding:

- the *Internet of Things* (IoT) expressing controllability of all system elements in the network,

- a widely spread *sensing* for collecting statuses of machines, materials and environment,

- *cyber-physical systems* (CPS) for automatic transmission and connection of all systems in one network, independently self-controlling, and

- the *Smart Factory* as final expression of self-controlling decentralized manufacturing processes in the value chain.

These essentially technical elements of Industry 4.0 are, for instance, equipped with regards to *business administrative and organizational* regards by Obermaier (2016, p. 8). To him, „Industry 4.0" is *one form of industrial value adding that is characterized by digitalization, automatization and connection of all actors participating along the value adding, and impinges on all processes, products and business models of industrial businesses.* He combines the technical and business administrative aspects which are reflected in the merger of the Office Floor and the Shop Floor for Wegener (2017, slide 8). The following business administrative and organizational elements therefore provide the gist of a digital/4.0 solution (hereto, see, for instance, the detailed discussion at BVL, 2017 a):

- operative *real time control* (de-coupling individual processes within the overall system),
- *customer individuality* of final products,
- *expanded objectives* (apart from a short throughput time through manufacturing, a high utilization of production facilities and low stocks within production, buffer times for establishing system flexibility are increasingly important),
- an extended *sensing* for data collection and
- *employee qualifications* (IT, processes).

By integrating cyber-physical systems into production and logistics, individual sub-steps of production can now be connected without media disruption. All system statuses are hereby permanently collected and provided to all relevant subsequent stages in real time. This warrants the data-technical transparency of all processes and statuses and allows availability to production planning and controlling. One further essential feature is the decentralized decision-making capacity of each system element. Hereto, value chains are connected horizontally (meaning all the stages of the chain) and vertically (meaning in all hierarchical steps of production planning and controlling). The cooperation within the supply chain ultimately changes fundamentally: *"Value adding is no longer happening sequentially and time-delayed, after all, but in a network of constantly communicating and flexibly inter-reacting units that widely organize themselves."* (Roland Berger, 2015, p. 17).

Indisputably, the implementation of Industry 4.0 is **entitled**: an increase in competitive advantages through increased customer benefit, increased flexibility and, respectively, through a decrease in costs. Maintaining the company's competitive position, in particular, is highlighted as an objective, in order to pre-empt being „ubered" overnight (the term „ubered" by Rolland Berger, 2015, p. 17).

Arranging it can be attached to the subordinate categories of Benefit of 4.0 concepts. For this purpose, there are several suggestions for discussion: **Porter/Heppelmann** (2015), for instance, differentiate four Benefit categories of 4.0 in their works Monitoring, Control, Optimization and Autonomy. Set against this, **Obermaier** (2016, p. 16ff.) emphasizes the effects of processes, products and future business models. Researchers of **acatech** identity the development of the value chain's agility as anchor point (Schuh et al., 2017, p. 7). The diversification of the features of agility is initiated by the acceleration of problem recognition, decisions and adaptation processes within value adding. Only this way, the benefits of real-time capable and cyber-physically connected machines and humans can be reaped. As examples, the following arrangements of realization by Schuh et al. (2017, p. 10) illustrated: faster decision processes, faster reaction to an increasing market dynamic of their customers, faster and more customer-specific development of new products and a shorter Time-to-Market. It becomes evident that, from Industry 4.0's perspective, »**time**«, as a factor, is the focus in all entrepreneurial processes. This goes not only for operative production processes, but also for individual processes in product development and the hierarchically company-internal coordination of the value adding.

In **conclusion** of characterizing Industry 4.0, it can be said that hereto, a *particular form of manufacturing organization* can be created in which (more) extensive data of the value chain can be used as additional information for flexible, autonomous and timely control and design of value adding. As concerns *technical requirements*, new developments of collection (i.e., sensing, data standards), transmission (i.e., horizontal and vertical networking to overcome media interruptions and interfaces) and processing (i.e., CPS, applications for analyzing and controlling the value chain) are deployed. As concerns *business administrative requirements*, particularly process organization, setting up relevant assessment criteria and their measurability, approaches to assess risks and their subsequent effects in the value chain, are to be tackled.

Set against this broadly definitional and future-oriented discussion, is a humbler **discussion of implementation**. Despite the, also international, connection of science, politics and economics, and the immense value adding potentials of Industry 4.0, the current state of implementation is still sobering. Schuh et al. put this in a nutshell: *"Realistically seen, potentials in the industrial reality of this range [note: 100 to 150 billion euros] still seem far away. [...] Merely singular pilots are now being implemented within companies which are rather in the nature of a technological feasibility study."* (Schuh et al., 2017, p.10). This is traced back to the *lack of benefit transparency* by the authors of acatech (p. 10).

c. Transferring of 4.0-elements to purchasing

The Industry 4.0 discussion serves as background and for better understanding of categorizing digital purchasing. Hereto, a detailed explanation can be found in my book „Digitale Transformation zum Einkauf 4.0. Nutzenbasierte Konzeptionen zum Smart Procurement" (Darr, 2017d). For a better understanding, a shortened illustration with regards to the research questions will be provided in the following.

Descriptions and delimitations of development stages in purchasing ranging from 1.0 to 4.0 build the starting point of a conception for Purchasing 4.0.

In the following, *Purchasing 1.0* refers to a personal purchasing order to a supplier. *Purchasing 2.0* refers, by analogy to Industry 2.0, to the routinizing of purchasing processes and goods replenishment, respectively. In *Purchasing 3.0*, that means the electric control of individual purchasing processes, goods replenishment is realized via just-in-time replenishment control or via eKanban. In *Purchasing 4.0*, analyses, decisions, control and transmission of purchasing processes, with reference to the attributes of Industry 4.0, are roughly executed, meaning automatic, connected, decentralized, in real time and (more) intelligent.

Business administrative and organizationally seen, *Purchasing 4.0* is defined as a *specific organizational form of order cycle, in which (more) extensive data of value adding and the environment can be used as additional information for a flexible, timely and autonomous control and design of purchasing management (i.e., its processes).* (Darr, 2017 d, p. 36).

Reflecting the work of Kagermann et al. (2012, p. 12), the technical design of this organization can be understood as follows: *The key element of Purchasing 4.0 is the intelligent organization of order processing - the smart procurement. It is characterized by a new intensity of socio-technical coordination between all actors and resources contributing to the purchasing order. The focus is on a connection of autonomous, situationally self-controlling, knowledge based, sensory supported and spatially distributed procurement resources (purchasing organization and suppliers within supply chain and production and logistics systems), including their planning, processing and control systems. Orders and procurement goods of Smart Procurement are unambiguously identifiable, localizable at any time and know their history, the current state, as well as alternative ways to the target state. This includes the products' way until the final end customer. All sensors within Smart Procurement provide their data as semantically described services that can be directly required by created components, products and the process environment.*

Like this, the forms of Purchasing 4.0 flow into one *Smart Procurement* (synonym: *Smart Purchasing*), which means in a digitally transformed organization of order cycle, the processes of which are thereby supposed to be self-controlling as last consequence. Individual elements obtain necessary data from processes and the environment which allows them to fulfill their tasks of examination and decision situationally and autonomously. By assessing existing historical data, prognoses for processing can be made which (can) trigger control within the process or flexible new planning.

In the basic logic of (purchasing) 4.0 concepts, the additional and timely availability of data is made usable for competition relevant findings in terms of better (smarter) decentralized planning and controlling decisions. The fact that every step along the value chain or within the order cycle is digitalized doesn't automatically mean that a high maturity level of Industry 4.0 should be assumed. Only from the connection of circumstances and their relevance for planning and controlling occurs a benefit. It was technical developments of data collection, storage, networking, processing and the possibilities of overcoming media interruptions (that means a change in media containing data), as well as managing interfaces (that means transferring data between applications), however, that have rendered these 4.0 discussions possible.

The discussion, explanation and conception of Purchasing 4.0, however, are not developed to that extent, either, albeit that corporate management places high requirements on purchasing: high efficiency (processes and purchasing services), additional effectiveness (new solutions by the supply chain) and strict observation of compliance or risk, respectively (guaranteeing legal requirements, conformity of processes and certainty of results).

Purchasing 4.0, however, is only mentioned subordinately in industrial discussions and does thus not yet seem to represent a prevailing application area from the viewpoint of Industry 4.0 discussions. Even the recently published study by Schuh et al. (2017, especially chapter 5) does not acknowledge purchasing as business function. Subsequently, purchasing is occasionally merely mentioned in sub-aspects in this acatech study: For example, purchasing is regarded as user of 4.0 applications (p.27). But, within the framework of the discussion of organizational structure (p. 9 ff.), or as component of the functional areas of a company (p.38ff.), purchasing is not mentioned.

As a further proof hereto, the results of a Google search (as of January 2019) are used:

- keyword *Industry 4.0*, ca. 372 million results,

- keyword *Procurement 4.0*, only ca. 20 million results,

- keyword *Einkauf 4.0*, ca. 12.4 million results.

Thereby, the state of implementation of Smart Procurement is unsurprisingly a similarly low standard as the state of implementation of Industry 4.0 (for implementation of Industry 4.0 see statements of Schuh et al., 2017). Hereto Bogaschewsky and Müller summarize the state of Purchasing 4.0 as follows:

"With regards to the topics electronic support of risk management within the supply chain and Industry 4.0, however, the situation is overall more than sobering. Despite all the hype about the topic of the Internet of things, companies and their

purchasing/SCM departments do scarcely have clear strategies, not to mention concrete applications to relevant extent. Moreover, anticipated applications focus on more or less evolutionary optimizations within existing systems, set against which, "disruptive innovations" seem only part of decision makers' imagination for the development of new business models etc. in exceptional cases." (Bogaschewsky/Müller, 2016, p.5).

Thereby, the wish and necessity of a digital purchasing is broadly discussed on the one hand, yet implementation is vague to open, meaning sobering (see for instance Deloitte, 2016). At this point (again, in analogy of Industry 4.0) the thesis is supported that the *lack of benefit transparency* presents an essential inhibition threshold for digital transformation. Empirical results of Bogaschewsky/Müller (2016, p. 4-5) prove this in detail.

It is therefore obvious that purchasing management has subsequently **not yet** become **an equal partner** of this digital value adding chain. This is another reason for overcoming the conceptional limits of benefit transparency and closing this described gap. This is done by differentiating the processes of the order cycle and of the information products.

d. Order cycle and information products as ground work of digital purchasing

In the following, two central fundaments of the Purchasing 4.0 conception are explained.

(1) The first fundament describes the operatively ongoing processes of the **order cycle**. Orders are defined as a trigger for a series of actions. The individual stages of which comprehend for finished products (i) the requirement-related order creation and transmission to suppliers, (ii) the supplier-related order processing,

(iii) the trigger actions and execution of the physical goods flow and (iv) handover actions to the client. The term "finished" relates to the closest customer of the supplier's, as is typical for make-to-stock processes. Figure 3.1 illustrates these four elements of the order cycle. There are examinations and decisions within each element. Figure 3.2 displays exemplarily the individual collection, examination and decision steps in detail and summarizes data that is to be individually collected, circumstances that are to be analyzed and decisions that are to be made for the order processing processes of finished products.

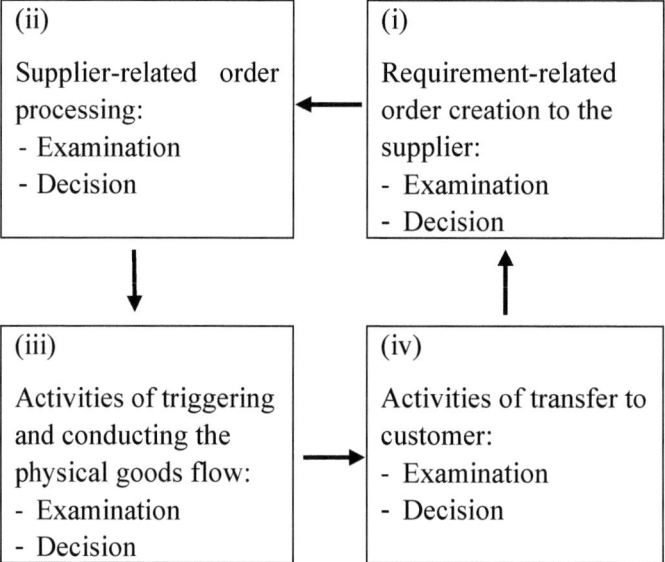

Figure 3.1: Basic structure of the order cycle

Process step	Collection	Analysis	Decision
Calculate gross requirement	Demand situation	Premises of the data basis	Confirmation of data situation
Inventory audit	Stock status	Accuracy of data	Confirmation of data situation
Calculate net requirements	Automated determination	Availability of data	Necessity of subsequent order
Determine order quantity	Necessary data	Availability of quantity	Alternative order quantity
Choose suppliers	Current offers	Comparison of suppliers	Choice of suppliers
Agree on prices	Current prices	Comparison of prices	Agreement of prices
Ordering	Necessary data	Completeness of data	Possible rework
Order confirmation	Order status	Completeness of confirmation	Possible rework
Delivery status monitoring	Permanent status	Conformity of limit values	Possible new control
Goods receipt	Determination of shipment	Alignment with order data	Possible review
Quality assurance	Determination of features	Alignment with agreement	Possible rejection
Goods collection	Determination of shipment	Completeness and correctness	Possible review
Storage	Inventory and quantity of delivery	Availability of space	Possible new choice of storage location
Process conformity	Process status	Alignment with limit values	Possible new control

Figure 3.2: Collection, analysis and decision within individual process steps of the order cycle

Here, it is to emphasize that *analyses* with regards to process safety and *decisions* for guaranteeing process safety occur with every process step. If the ordering, for instance, is conducted without complete data, a subsequent amendment may be necessary that would affect process safety. The same goes for quantity determination over choice of suppliers to storage.

For more customer individual products (or components, respectively), for example, within the framework of assemble to order or make to order, the order cycle is extended by production planning, production controlling and, if necessary, product development at the supplier's site. This possibility is not further regarded in this work.

Individual stages of the order cycle are to be conducted equally within the framework of traditional purchasing concepts and also after a digital transformation, even if the implementation of collecting statuses, the analysis of statuses and the recommended decisions (should) turn out differently.

(2) The second pillar addresses individual stages (**maturity levels**) of digitalization. The systemization of maturity levels for a more distinct division of concept implementations is nothing new. Such proposals have been made for digital purchasing, as well.

The **BVL** (2017b, p. 46) has differentiated three levels in total in **their** approach: The *descriptive* level (What happened? Description of the situation), the *predictive* level (What is going to happen? Extrapolation and prognosis) and the *prescriptive* (normative) level (What should be realized? Recommendation of action).

The second proposal originates from Schuh et al. (2017, p. 16) and **Schuh et al.** (2016). Conversely, they differentiate *six maturity levels* in total. The first two stages thereby describe the prerequisites of digitalization, through computerization and its interconnectivity. Based on this groundwork, further maturity levels are identified as visibility (level 3: what is happening?), transparency (level 4: why is it happening?), prognostic capacity (level 5: what is going to happen?) and adaptivity (level 6: how to react autonomously?).

These two proposals are similar in a certain way. This work follows Schuh's et al. (2017) classification, since their distinction into collection, analysis and decision has been made more clearly. Contrary to Schuh et al., the terminology, however, is adapted: The terms '(sensory) collection' or 'analysis', respectively, are preferred because the terms 'visibility' or 'transparency' are linguistically too close to each other:

-   The first level is *sensory collection* and forwarding of circumstances and statuses. Furthermore, the type of data to be collected and the type of forwarding are attributed to this level. Here, collection and transmission (forwarding) are conceptually summarized, since they only make sense when combined. This level includes the data collection.

-   The second level is *analyzing*/processing these circumstances in the sense of preparing control, planning or decision. This level includes data processing.

-   The third level includes a (*agile/self-controlling*) decision against the background of collected and analyzed circumstances. This level contains the triggering or, respectively, the controlling of processes and, possibly, the implementation of plans, concepts or strategies.

Insofar, the proposed maturity levels correspond to the factually logical procedure of data management within the decision process: from collecting/storing necessary data over their processing/analyzing to the final decision.

The collection of all circumstances in the shape of data sets the foundation for a so-called digital shadow, whose existence in itself is worthless. It obtains worth, that means a benefit, only through certain attributes. In order to emphasize the difference between data and their benefit linguistically, it is referred to an **informatory product**. The digital shadow builds the necessary foundation for the informatory products. They describe attributes which have been created (meaning produced) in the course of data processing and are defined from the benefit for the participants within the order cycle. There are **four information products** distinguished in total. They are derived from the four possible levels of a service (hereto see, for instance, Weber, 2012, p. 139):

- the provisioning as a service (level 1),
- the conduction of processes as a service (level 2),
- the result of the processes as a service and
- the effect on customers as a service (level 4).

The parallelism of the individually mentioned maturity levels to the first three levels of a service is evident: providing data corresponds to collecting/storing, implementing to processing and the decision corresponds to the result. Yet, in this benefit-based work, four and not three information products are distinguished because the effect of a decision shall be considered separately from the decision. Furthermore, by considering the informatory product, the *benefit-related performance features* are expressed more clearly than when viewed through collection, analysis or, respectively, decision (in an input-related way). The looked at four information products (IP) are specifically:

- **Information product 1**: The provision of data describes the first level. The existence of data is identified as "machine-readably documented, or rather *documented*". The circumstances of the process (or process step, respectively) are documented with regards to relevant features in machine readable form and can be timely evaluated with regards to these features. The reason or rather rationale behind the documentation of individual processes or their states, respectively, can be found in the necessity of providing relevant data for the particular data user for further process steps within the order cycle (information recipient). Therefore, informatory product 1 is only a derivative product. The specific scope of relevant data to be collected is to be determined for the individual user within the order cycle.

The service provided by information product 1 is hereby its possibility for a timely and individually situative provision of historical data, for example, for reasons of context specific evaluation, decision preparation or decision making, respectively.

- **Information product 2**: Assessing the quality of process conduct is what describes the second information product. It is classified as *"examined"*. This process (respectively process step) is then evaluated with regards to determined features, that means examined. The reason or rather rationale behind the examination of individual processes/states can be found in the safety to continue or release subsequent process steps without having to bear risks from ongoing or upstream steps. The scope of examinations and respective relevant examination criteria are to be defined for each specific step within the order cycle.

The service of information product 2 can hereby be attributed to (traceably) safeguarding the quality of upstream and ongoing informatory, material or spatially-temporary process performance. Generally, information product 2 is based on information product 1 (collection and storage).

- **Information product 3**: The third step describes the process result and is defined as *"decided"*. The process (or sequence of process steps, respectively) has been determined, that means decided upon. The reason or rather rationale behind a decision can be found in the result conform continuation or determination of subsequent steps within the value adding/order processing. The scope of decisions and the respective relevant data basics are to be determined for each specific order cycle.

- Information product 3: The third step describes the process result and is defined as "decided". The process (or sequence of process steps, respectively) has been determined, that means decided upon. The reason or rather rationale behind a decision can be found in the result conform continuation or determination of subsequent steps within the value adding/order processing. The scope of decisions and the respective relevant data basics are to be determined for each specific order cycle.

- **Information product 4**: The fourth level describes the benefit for following users within the process and is identified as *"effective"*. The process (or sequence of steps, respectively) has valid impacts on purchasing or suppliers, i.e. in the shape of guaranteed deadline compliance or stable order receipts. Another example of information product 4 is the possibility of tracing back analyses and decisions. The service is herein placed in the chance for timely subsequent verification and analysis (i) of the documentation of relevant features of the value adding process, (ii) the performed examinations and (iii) the decisions made for continuing and controlling processes or value adding, respectively. The scope of documented data of processes, statuses, analyses and decisions are defined (limited) by the opportunities of traceability.

- The service of this information product can be found basically in providing benefit in the sense of operative and strategic objectives for the organization. This goes for purchasing, as well as for the supplier. Information product 4 is generally based on information product 3 (decision). In this work, process, result and customer benefit have been distinguished previously as basic and potential benefit categories. The remaining part of this work builds on this foundation.

e. Digital Penetration Point as structural feature of the level of digitalization

The technically characterized maturity levels, that are also expressed in information products (IP) 1 to 3, are only effective through a benefit assessment by the recipient, that means in information product 4. Therefore, information product 4 always represents the starting point for thoughts about implementing a maturity level. **Retrogradely**, information product 3 (effective decisions), information product 2 (relevant and necessary analyses and their data requirements) and product 1 (scope of relevant data and their collection, storage and transmission) can be determined and implemented. This chain of 4 to 1 is always to be considered as a whole. It also makes sense to think of the four levels 'starting from the end' instead of technically going through the sequence of maturity levels 1 to 3. This is done separately for process, result and customer benefit.

Individual information products are to be brought in accordance with each other independently of their arrangements. Thereby, all four levels or only the first/first two/first three information products may be 'digitalized'. The border between digital and analogue (that means stages within the order cycle conducted by employees) world is identified as **Digital Penetration Point (DPP)**. This point describes to what extent the processes within the order cycle are shaped by interconnected, autonomous, self-controlling, knowledge based, sensory supported and spatially distributed resources.

Depending on the arrangement of digitalization, the states 0, 1, 2, 3 and 4 are distinguished. This is to be done for each benefit category 'necessary', 'important' and 'strategic':

- Within **state 0,** the DPP is situated "prior to the process chain", which means that the data are incomplete or not available in machine readable form. By the same token, there are no further steps in terms of digital information products.

- Within **state 1**, at least the data are completely and mechanically available. However, evaluating or decision preparation, respectively, is only done manually.

- Within **state 2**, data are evaluated by means of algorithms. However, the decision proposal is still made manually.

- Within **state 3**, the decision proposal is made by a software application. A broadly known example (not from purchasing) would be a passenger car's navigation system that assesses destination, current location, traffic situation and prognosis for punctuality in real time; and if needed, proposes alternative routes.

- And within **state 4**, this proposal is executed via application. There is no need for manual intervention.

Figure 3.3 shows the different states 0 to 4 and their Digital Penetration Points in the form of a red stepped parting line. The activities of purchasing within the individual stages of the order cycle (see figure 3.1), from the collection of necessary data to the decision, are conducted via applications in the digital world (red) and the transmission of results from one stage to the next, that means overcoming the interface, is done by applications, as well. In figure 3.3, they are indicated by blue arrow symbols. In the analogue world (black), interfaces and media interruptions are bridged by manual activities (black arrow symbols).

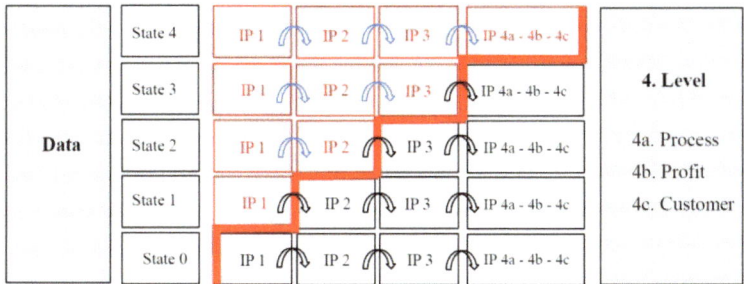

Figure 3.3: Digital Penetration Points

The data organization within the order cycle is based on the succession of collection, examination and decision sequences between purchasing and suppliers. Data processing activities distinguish collection, analysis and decision. The hereby necessary data requirement of each process step defines the place of collection, the documentation in master data or transaction data, the arrangement of data or, respectively, information supply and the transmission to a data pool. The digital world opens up additional opportunities for analysis and decision due to further documented data. Hereto, requirements for a consistent data model are to be fulfilled for every process step within the order cycle. The provision of relevant data for examinations (analyses) and decisions are to be safeguarded, as well. Figure 3.4 jointly displays these elements in the (digital) order cycle.

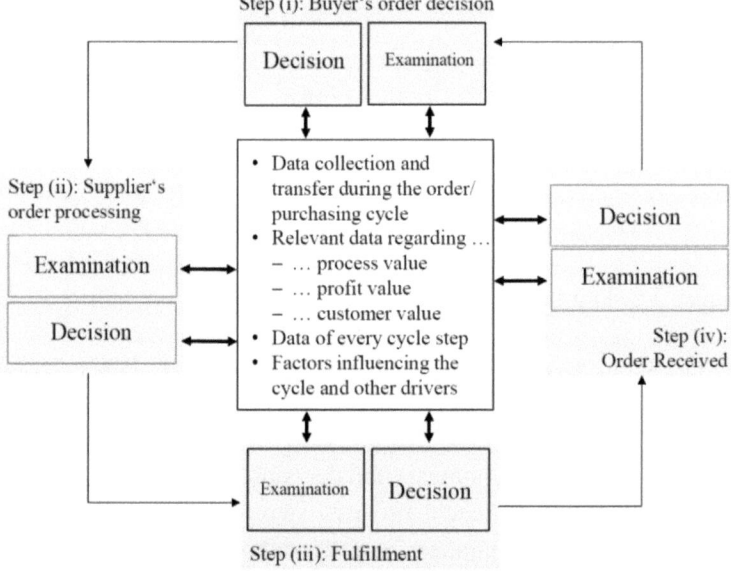

Figure 3.4: Data organization within the order cycle

f. Second interim conclusion

The consideration of the digitalization of purchasing (Purchasing 4.0) is treated specifically with regards to the three benefit levels "process/necessary", "result/important" and "customer/strategic". It is to be examined on a case-by-case basis to what extent digitalization has been implemented within a company, that means where the Digital Penetration Point lies. By doing so, each company can be attributed one state 0, 1, 2, 3 or 4.

4. Exemplary purchasing profiles

a. Display of profiles of Procurement Excellence

The performance capability of purchasing is portrayed with regards to the explained characteristics. It is documented via three tables:

- The 3x3 matrix as performance profile of purchasing with table 4.1 as pattern of results 1

- KPIs for controlling purchasing services with table 4.2 as pattern of results 2

- Location of the Digital Penetration Point with table 4.3 as pattern of results 3

3x3 matrix		User (R)		
		Purchasing	Production	Sales
Benefit (N)	strategic (s)	7. Strategically important services for purchasing	8. Strategically important services for production	9. Strategically important services for sales
	important (w)	4. Important services for purchasing	5. Important services for production	6. Important services for sales
	necessary (n)	1. Necessary services for purchasing	2. Necessary services for production	3. Necessary services for sales

Table 4.1: Profile of purchasing services

User (R) / Benefit (N)	Purchasing	Production	Sales
Customer (s) strategic	• Purchasing and strategic	• Production and strategic	• Sales and strategic
Earnings (w) important	• Purchasing and important	• Production and important	• Sales and important
Process (n) necessary	• Purchasing and necessary	• Production and necessary	• Sales and necessary

Table 4.2: KPIs for controlling the service profile

	IP 1	IP 2	IP 3	IP 4
State 4				n, w, s
State 3				n, w, s
State 2				n, w, s
State 1				n, w, s
State 0				n, w, s
Information product (IP)	IP 1	IP 2	IP 3	IP 4

Table 4.3: Location of the Digital Penetration Point

b. Depiction of case A

Case A represents a typical performance profile of purchasing: Fields 1, 2, 4 and 5 (see table 4.4) are covered by purchasing services. Fields 1 and 2 are necessary components of the business model. Replenishment control until production is managed actively. Purchasing prices and possible risks on the suppliers' side are actively analyzed and proactively evaluated. By doing so, purchasing contributes to securing earnings.

Services on parts of sales (fields 3, 6 or 9) are not what purchasing focuses on and thus not dealt with. Likewise, strategic services of purchasing (fields 7 to 9), that means contributions to positioning the company in the sales market, are not realized.

Thereby it becomes clear that the company's replenishment safety is the focus and that these decisions are made vis-à-vis costs and risks.

3x3 matrix		User		
		Purchasing	Production	Sales
Benefit	strategic	7	8	9
	important	4	5	6
	necessary	1	2	3

Table 4.4: A: Profile of the purchasing service

These comprehensive services are controlled by the help of KPIs (see table 4.5). There are process key figures (necessary benefit) in terms of quality, delivery time and stocks. There are result-related key figures (important benefit) or indicators with regards to procurement prices, procurement risks and avoidance of additional costs for production. They can be expressed by target-actual comparisons within the framework of budget controlling.

Key figures that display strategic and/or sales-related services are not available.

User (R) / Benefit (N)	Purchasing	Production	Sales
Customer (strategic)	• not available	• not available	• not available
Earnings (important)	• price developments • risks • quality assurance	• stability of production planning	• not available
Process (necessary)	• delivery time • quality • stocks	• quality • stocks	• not available

Table 4.5: A: KPIs for controlling the service profile

Decisions that are to be made can be proactively kicked off and initiated because of the KPIs. The hereto needed data of processes and effects of earnings are procured from different sources (ERP data, suppliers, market data amongst others) and mechanically processed. Thereby, proactive actions and their preparation is institutionalized.

The location of the Digital Penetration Point is described by state 2 (see table 4.6). Organizing data for the decisions to be made is the result of a controlled process: data procurement, data examination, data processing in the sense of process safety and the effects of earnings.

	IP 1	IP 2	IP 3	IP 4
State 4				
State 3				
State 2	n and w	n and w		
State 1				
State 0				

Table 4.6: A: Position of the Digital Penetration Point

The initiative of individual purchasers is coined by this implemented data organization. The responsible parties know about the purchasers' support for their tasks.

In conclusion, it is to be determined that with a recently growing acceptance of purchasing's strategic role, investments in controlling and support tools have been made. Introducing a software for a corporation-wide enterprise resource planning (ERP) and a deliberate data management in compliance with the two purchasing services sets the necessary first step hereto.

c. Depiction of case B

From today's point of view, case B represents the maximum service spectrum: all nine fields are actively perceived as fields of activity.

3x3 matrix		User		
		Purchasing	Production	Sales
Benefit	strategic	7	8	9
	important	4	5	6
	necessary	1	2	3

Table 4.7: B: Profile of the purchasing service

User (R) / Benefit (N)	Purchasing	Production	Sales
Customer (strategic)	• project performance • flexible process service	• project performance • access to production technologies	• project performance • innovative supplier service
Earnings (important)	• Quality • Process costs • Material costs • Risks	• Quality • Process costs • Risks	• Quality • Process costs Risks
Process (necessary)	• Purchasing KPIs • Delivery time, stocks • Process safety	• Production KPIs • Stocks • Lead time	• KPIs of sales • Stocks • Delivery

Table 4.8: B: KPIs for controlling the service profile

The process controlling of materials and goods is executed consistently from suppliers to customers. Fluctuations in customer demand are caught and secured by a capable network of suppliers. The effects of earnings are proactively analyzed in total and evaluated in real time in terms of risks. The purchasing company's market position is actively affected by innovative product and process services. This can be expressed by 'value improvement projects' which are initiated on part of sales out of quality, risk, cost or, respectively, customers' process projects. On a strategic level, long term customer projects give impetus for process, quality and cost objectives of the purchasing department.

The KPIs for controlling the service profile can be defined as consistent. Process services in the three areas are each documented via specific key figures (target and actual). Likewise, for cost and risk analyses, especially for material prices, there are continual evaluations. These also serve as foundation for rolling planning. For strategic projects of the value improvement, KPIs serve to track individual work steps (of purchasing as well).

State 4				
State 3	n, w, s	n, w, s	n, w, s	
State 2				
State 1				
State 0 (strategic)				
	IP 1	IP 2	IP 3	IP 4

Table 4.9: B: Location of the Digital Penetration Point

The comprehensive purchasing services and worked out KPIs are also expressed by the location of the Digital Penetration Point (see table 4.9). For internal process services of purchasing data-related requirements, comparing analyses for decision preparation from the production orders and the decision proposal for purchasing are already established in a digitally integrated form.

The final decision and its implementation are, however, not left to an application.

Key figures of important services are proactively and decision preparatorily reprocessed. Key figures for strategic questions as well are collected, analyzed and prepared as decision template in an automated way. Data control from suppliers to customers is managed in a digital way.

In conclusion, it is to be determined that the services of purchasing comprehend all fields. There is digital support available in the control for processes and earnings/risks. Internally, there is digital integration. For the strategic services (USP), an effective degree of digitalization is reached as well.

d. Depiction of case C

The service profile of case C (see table 4.10) is a historical review and serves as comparison to case B. Purchasing services concentrate on a punctual provision of raw materials and supply parts (fields 1 and 2). Purchasing decisions are also made (»on-the-spot«) against the background of comparing procurement prices (4). Proactive elements about the markets are missing. There are no sales-related purchasing services; by the same, there is no support for analyzing the earnings situation in production and for strategic services.

In case C, the controlling through key figures is focused on the order triggering and completion (see table 4.11). In terms of supply parts, there are a frequent KPI supported and manual stock analyses and a manually comparing evaluation of prices. Services for production focus on a sufficing provision of supply parts for short term production planning.

3x3 matrix		User		
		Purchasing	Production	Sales
Benefit	strategic	7	8	9
	important	4	5	6
	necessary	1	2	3

Table 4.10: C: Profile of the purchasing service

The location of the Digital Penetration Point (see table 4.12) is described by state 0, since production demand and inventories are available in different data sources. Software based proposals for quantitative procurement cannot be generated. The purchasing decision is rather made by purchasing on the basis of their "personal" data organization and initiative.

User (R) / Benefit (N)	Purchasing	Production	Sales
Customer (strategic)	• not available	• not available	• not available
Earnings (important)	• Purchasing price comparisons	• not available	• not available
Process (necessary)	• Reorder level of stocks • Delivery time	• Short-term production plan	• not available

Table 4.11: C: KPIs for controlling the service profile

Decisions to be made are then prepared based on manual initiatives (day-to-day business, appointments or others). Hereto necessary data are then procured from different sources (ERP data amongst others) and further processed. Proactive actions and their preparation are not institutionalized.

In total, purchasing in case C is very traditionally oriented; KPIs for controlling are based on order completion and safeguarding goods availability for production. Data procurement and processing are responsibilities of the purchaser. The degree of digitalization here only reaches state 0.

	IP 1	IP 2	IP 3	IP 4
State 4				
State 3				
State 2				
State 1				
State 0				

Table 4.12: C: Location of the Digital Penetration Point

5. Procurement Excellence of type 1 and type 2

a. Procurement Excellence in terms of service extent (type1)

The arrangement of excellent purchasing management has two dimensions: for one, a powerful arrangement with regards to its importance for the company. Here, purchasing makes its first excellent contribution. This is defined as **type 1**. It is expressed in the characteristics of purchasing service benefit for the purchasing company. Necessary services, that means process services, set the basis of a functioning business model; important services support in terms of earnings- and risk-related effects of purchasing decisions; strategic services help profile the company (significantly) in the sales market. The higher the benefit for the company the higher the extent of excellence of type 1 is classified. Therefore, a strategic service is the highest level of Procurement Excellence of type 1.

Table 5.1 shows the classification of the first type of Procurement Excellence for the three cases. It is clear to say that one level of Excellence is covered at a time. Case A (category "important") can still be improved through purchasing in terms of contribution to the company by working out specific services of the supplier network for the company's own market profiling. Exclusive product services or service features for a better market position/market development can be named as examples. Possibly needed requirements in purchasing hereto, for instance in qualified human or physical resources, are to be created beforehand.

In case C, a fundamental decision concerning the extension of purchasing services is due: The value contribution of purchasing in the company is to be made clear, and the data organization is to be determined in terms of processes and earnings/risks.

Procurement Excellence type 1	Example
Necessary services: process services	Case C
Important services: earnings and risk	Case A
Strategic services: USP in the sales market	Case B

Table 5.1: Procurement Excellence type 1

In case B (category "strategic"), the company can basically improve by refining and expanding its services of the supply network. Furthermore, this head start is to be secured with regards to active competitors.

b. Procurement Excellence vis-à-vis management quality (type 2)

On the other hand, as a high level management service, purchasing management can be significant for the company. Here, purchasing makes a second excellent contribution. This is expressed by the quality of purchasing management and constitutes the second dimension of Procurement Excellence (**type 2**).

The attempt to categorize this on the foundation of personalized dimensions of management quality is not pursued in this work. A high degree of personal commitment, a strong willingness to commit or consequent ambition to follow corporate interests by purchasers shall in no case be questioned. Here, management quality is only defined by visible and examinable features, that means management shows observable circumstances of how planning, controlling and monitoring are conducted.

Visible signs include available KPIs on the one hand, so that purchasers work with tools to better assess situations and better prepare or, respectively, make decisions. On the other hand, visible signs include rapidness and extent of provided data and applications for extracting information from data. A higher state of digitalization or rather a greater extent of information products paves the way for more comprehensively prepared, faster and more effective decisions.

Three categories of Excellence of type 2 are defined by '**standard**', '**advanced**' and '**excellent**'. 'Standard' categories include missing proactive KPIs, the struggles of generating information (from analyses), that means state 0 or 1. 'Advanced' categories include individual proactive KPIs for support, namely the consistency of goods control within the company and state 2. 'Excellent' categories include comprehensive proactive KPIs and a high degree of digitalization (state 3 or 4). Table 5.2 ranks the three cases: Case C provides little/scarce tools and is classified as 'standard'. Case A is classified as 'advanced' and case B as 'excellent'.

Procurement Excellence type 2	Example
Standard: personal decisions	Case C
Advanced: organization & efficiency	Case A
Excellent: learning and sustainability	Case B

Table 5.2: Procurement Excellence type 2

These classifications of companies now contain **starting points for improving** management capabilities of purchasers. A first step for companies of the category 'standard' would be to create (or expand, respectively) an effective purchasing controlling (data basis and KPIs) in order to obtain relevant findings about their own service performance in time. This also includes benefit-related processing of the purchasing and replenishment situation of procurement prices and risks. In both cases, corporate data and software-related requirements are to be created.

For all 'advanced' companies, the question furthermore arises to what extent improving the Digital Penetration Point should be considered a current challenge, that means to what extent they further digitalize their purchasing processes. This surpasses creating a purchasing controlling by far. Because to do so, purchasing processes in the company and with the suppliers are, if needed, to be newly designed and developed with regards to information products in a 'documented', 'analyzed', 'decided' and 'effective' way. Thereby, the question that arises vis-à-vis digital developments is not 'If' but 'When'. The state 'Excellent' now still remains to be further expanded or secured, respectively.

c. Procurement Excellence: Integration of dimensions

The integration of the two types of Procurement Excellence is done in table 5.3, in a **3x3 matrix**. Categorizing each particular company via types 1 and 2 equally brings up- and downsides from the methodological point of view: On the one hand, through a rougher positioning, a more robust recommendation of action can be given. This simplification neglects individual aspects without, however, changing the gist of the message. That is the thought. On the other hand, a latent danger exists that in doing so, essential correlations will be lost and therefore the quality of the reason for an impact direction affected. In any case, awareness is raised for this important question in corporate leadership and suggestions for internal discussions are made.

Field A1 sets the starting point of the development, that means a necessary purchasing service with a 'standard' execution quality. A first impulse direction occurs in terms of benefit of the purchasing services. Reaching field B1 is defined as stopover "result". Set against this, field **C1** opens up to strategically seizing the chances within the supply chain.

3x3 matrix of Procurement Excellence		Excellence with regards to management (type 2)		
		Standard (1)	Advanced (2)	Excellent (3)
Excellence with regards to purchasing service benefit (type 1)	Level A necessary	A1 starting point	A2 stopover "efficiency"	A3 impulse direction „sustainable management"
	Level B important	B1 stopover "earnings"	B2	B3
	Level C strategic	C1 impulse direction "chances of the supply chain"	C2	C3 impulse direction "sustainable and strategic"

Table 5.3: 3x3 matrix of Procurement Excellence

A second impulse direction of development is initiated with regards to an increase in management quality. Reaching field A2 is defined as stopover "efficiency", and the steepest rise occurs in field **A3** "sustainable management". In the column 'Excellent', opportunities of digitalization for purchasing decisions are used to full extent. The best case **(C3)** boasts a sustainable and strategic purchasing management which (pro-) actively uses the strategic chances of the supply chain and supports each particular decision in an effective way through excellent information products.

The three exemplary cases can eventually be classified into this 3x3 matrix as follows:

- Case **A** in field **B2**: Important Services & Advanced

- Case **B** in field **C3**: Strategic Services & Excellent

- Case **C** in field **A1**: Necessary Services & Standard

These three examples have been chosen out of didactic reasons and serve the examination and discussion of interested readers.

d. Conclusion

The service capability of purchasing or its purchasers, respectively, is nowadays a great opportunity to secure one's own competitiveness and sustainable profitability. Procurement Excellence is a reasonable claim to today's corporate leadership. For the design and active influencing on parts of the company's leadership, there is a need for concrete concepts, in order to illustrate and assess the current status and possible impulses.

In this work, a foundation (i) of conceptions towards user/ benefit and (ii) of conceptions towards information products/ Digital Penetration Point are explained and discussed via three case studies.

Thank you for your interest.

6. Bibliography

Baily, P.; Farmer, D.; Crocker, B.; Jessop, D.; Jones, D. (2015): Procurement Principles and Management, 11. Aufl., Pearson, Harlow 2015

Batran, A.; Erben, A.; Schulz, R.; Sperl, F. (2017): Procurement 4.0. A Survival Guide in a Disruptive World, Frankfurt/New York 2017

Bogaschewsky, Ronald; Müller, Holger (2016): Industrie 4.0: Wie verändern sich die IT-Systeme in Einkauf und SCM, in Zusammenarbeit mit Bundesverband Materialwirtschaft, Einkauf und Logistik e. V. (BME) und Bundesverband Materialwirtschaft, Einkauf und Logistik in Österreich (BMÖ), Würzburg/Leipzig 2016

BVL (2017a): Logistik als Wissenschaft – zentrale Forderungen in Zeiten der vierten industriellen Revolution. Positionspapier des Wissenschaftlichen Beirats der Bundesvereinigung Logistik e. V. (BVL), Bremen 2017

BVL (2017b): Trends und Strategien in Logistik und Supply Chain Management, Bremen 2017

Chui, M.; Manyika, J.; Miremadi, M. (2016): Where machines could replace humans - and where they can't (yet), in: McKinsey Quarterly, July 2016, S. 1-12

Darr, W. (1992): Integrierte Marketing-Logistik, Wiesbaden 1992

Darr, W. (2017a): Grundfragen des Einkaufsmanagements, Hamburg 2017

Darr, W. (2017 b): Spezialfragen des Einkaufsmanagements, Hamburg 2017

Darr, W. (2017 c): Betriebswirtschaftliche Konzept im Lichte der Rationalität. Homo oeconomicus - Optimierung - Effizienz - Supply Chain Management - Lokale Cluster - Unternehmens- strategien - Selbstorganisation, Hamburg 2017

Darr, W. (2017 d): Digitale Transformation zum Einkauf 4.0. Nutzenbasierte Konzeptionen zum Smart Procurement, Hamburg 2017

Darr, W. (2019): Advanced Issues of Procurement Management, Hamburg 2019

Deloitte (2016): Operations Insights: Digitalisierung im Einkauf. Bausteine einer digitalen Strategie für den Einkauf, https://www2.deloitte.com/content/dam/Deloitte/de/Docume nts/operations/Digitalisierung%20Einkauf_04- 2016_safe.pdf, (Retrieved on: 15.10.2017)

Deloitte (2017): The Deloitte Global Chief Procurement Officer Survey 2017: Growth: the cost and digital imperative, London 2017, https://www2.deloitte.com/mm/en/pages/operations/articles/c po-survey-2017.html, (Retrieved on: 15.10.2017)

Entchelmeier, A. (2008): Supply Performance Management. Leistungsmessung in Einkauf und Supply Management, Wiesbaden 2008

Frey, Carl B.; Osborne, Michael A. (2013): Future of employment. How susceptible are jobs to computerisation, Oxford 2013, in: www.oxfordmartin.ox.ac.uk/downloads/academic/The_Futur e_of_Employment.pdf , (Retrieved on: 18.09.2017)

Hausladen, Iris (2016): IT-gestützte Logistik, Systeme - Prozesse - Anwendungen, 3. Aufl., Wiesbaden 2016

Heß, Gerhard (2010): Supply-Strategien in Einkauf und Beschaffung, 2. Aufl., Wiesbaden 2010

Hofstetter, Y. (2016): Ende der Demokratie, München 2016

Johnson, P.; Leenders, M.; Flynn, A. (2011): Purchasing and Supply Management, 14th Edition, McGraw Hill International Edition 2011

Kagermann, H.; Wahlster, H.; Helbig, J. (2012): Umsetzungsempfehlungen für das Zukunftsprojekt Industrie 4.0. Deutschlands Zukunft als Produktionsstandort sichern, Abschlussbericht des Arbeitskreises Industrie 4.0, Promotorengruppe Kommunikation der Forschungsunion Wirtschaft, Hrsg.: H. Kagermann, W. Wahlster, J. Helbig, Berlin 2012. (In der Endfassung 2013 erschienen)

Kim, W. C.; Mauborgne, R. (2005): Der blaue Ozean als Strategie. Wie man neue Märkte schafft, München 2005

Krampf, Peter (2014): Beschaffungsmanagement, 2. Aufl., München 2014

Krauskopf, Sinja (2017): Der kluge Einkauf - Was ist Einkauf 4.0?, http://www.vandermeergruppe.de/der-kluge-einkauf-einkauf-4-0/ (Retrieved on: 29.04.2017)

Kreutzer, Ralf; Land K.-H. (2015): Dematerialisierung - Die Neuverteilung der Welt in Zeiten des digitalen Darwinismus, Köln: Futurevisionpress 2015

Kreutzer, Ralf; Neugebauer, Tim; Pattloch, Annette (2017): Digital Business Leadership: Digitale Transformation – Geschäftsmodell-Innovation – agile Organisation – Change-Management, Wiesbaden 2017

Large, Rudolf (2014): Strategisches Beschaffungsmanagement, 4. Aufl., Wiesbaden 2014

Lysons, K.; Farrington, B. (2012): Purchasing and Supply Chain Management, Pearson Education, London 2012

Mühlberger, Annette (2017): Auf die Plätze, fertig, vernetzt!, in: Best in Procurement, Vol. 8, Heft 3, 2017, S. 14-17

Obermaier, Robert (2016): Industrie 4.0 als unternehmerische Gestaltungsaufgabe: Strategische und operative Handlungsfelder für Industriebetriebe, in: Industrie 4.0 als unternehmerische Gestaltungsaufgabe. Betriebswirtschaftliche, technische und rechtliche Herausforderungen, Hrsg.: R. Obermaier, Wiesbaden 2016, S. 3-34

Otto, Andreas (2003): Supply Chain Event Management, in: International Journal of Logistics Management, Vol. 14, Iss. 2, 2003, S. 1-13

O.V. (2017a): Digitalisierung erfordert konsequenten Wandel, in: Log.Letter 4/2017, S. 2-3

O.V. (2017b): Nachholbedarf im E-Procurement, in: Best in Procurement, Vol. 8, Heft 3, 2017, S. 6

Pellengahr, Karolin; Schulte, Axel; Richard, Judith; Berg, Matthias (2016): Vorstudie Einkauf 4.0. Digitalisierung des Einkaufs, Hrsg.: Fraunhofer-Institut für Materialfluss und Logistik IML und Bundesverband Materialwirtschaft, Einkauf und Logistik e.V. (BME), Dortmund/ Frankfurt 2016

Picot, A.; Reichwald, R.; Wigand, R. (2003): Die grenzenlose Unternehmung. Information, Organisation und Management, 5. Auflage, Wiesbaden 2003

Porter, M. (1980): Competitive Strategy: Techniques for Analyzing Industries and Competitors, New York: Free Press 1980

Porter, M.; Heppelmann, J. E. (2015): How Smart, Connected Products Are Transforming Companies, in: Harvard Business Review, Vol. 93, Iss. 10, Oct. 2015, S. 97-114

Postman, Neil (1992): Das Technopol, Frankfurt am Main 1992

PwC (2014): Industrie 4.0 – Chancen und Herausforderungen der vierten industriellen Revolution, www.strategyand.pwc.com/reports/industrie-4-0, (Retrieved on: 07.06.2017)

Roland Berger (2015): Die digitale Transformation der Industrie. Studie im Auftrag des Bundesverbandes der Deutschen Industrie e. V., Berlin 2015, www.bdi.eu/media/user_upload/Digitale_Transformation.pdf, (Retrieved on: 07.06.2017)

Roth, A. (2016): Einführung und Umsetzung von Industrie 4.0, Hrsg.: A. Roth, Berlin/ Heidelberg 2016

Schuh, G.; Blum, M.; Reschke, J.; Birkmeier, M. (2016): Der Digitale Schatten in der Auftragsabwicklung, in: Zeitschrift für wirtschaftlichen Fabrikbetrieb (ZWF), Jg. 111, H. 1-2, 2016, S. 48-51

Schuh, G., Anderl, R., Gausemeier J., ten Hompel, M., Wahlster, W. (2017), (Hrsg.): Industrie 4.0 Maturity Index. Die digitale Transformation von Unternehmen gestalten, (acatech STUDIE), München 2017

Taleb, Nassim (2008): Schwarze Schwäne, München 2008

van Weele, A.J. (2014): Purchasing and Supply Chain Management: Analysis, Strategy, Planning & Practice, 6th Edition, Cengage Learning, EMEA 2014

van Weele, Arjan J.; Eßig, Michael (2017): Strategische Beschaffung, Wiesbaden 2017

vom Brocke, Jan; Schmiedel, Theresa; Recker, Jan; Trkman, Peter; Mertens, Willem; Viaene, Stijn (2014): Ten principles of good business process management, in: Business Process Management Journal, Vol. 20, Issue 4, 2014, S. 530-548

Weber, Jürgen (2012): Logistikkostenrechnung, 3. Aufl., Berlin/Heidelberg 2012

Wegener, Dieter (2017): „Industrie 4.0" – wie die Digitalisierung die Produktionskette revolutioniert, Vortrag auf der 3. INDIGO-Konferenz „Digitale Produktion" an der OTH Amberg-Weiden am 30. Juni 2017

Wolter, Marc Ingo et al. (2015): Industrie 4.0 und die Folgen für Arbeitsmarkt und Wirtschaft. Szenario-Rechnungen im Rahmen der BIBB-IAB-Qualifikations- und Berufsfeldprojektionen, Hrsg.: Institut zur Arbeitsmarkt- und Berufsforschung der Bundesagentur für Arbeit, IAB Forschungsbericht 8/2015, Nürnberg 2015